Poetry From The Unknown

Poetry From The Unknown

JLynn

Dedicated - "To The One Who Freed Me."

Preface

I never thought I'd be here. When I first started, I was lost. I just wanted to be a better communicator. I had so much to say, so many feelings, and nowhere to put it. Journaling, what a concept. I honestly never meant to share it with anyone. Those in my circle just wouldn't let it go. You can do it, they said. Here's your front row seat to what goes on in my head. These are my most intimate and private thoughts. I am happy and excited for you to get to know me and my work. ENJOY!

JL Mitchell

Let me set the scene for you

Its 1989, a third grader finds herself anxiously waiting for class to begin... there were four rows of five desks... she sat in the front, on the inside aisle... here she discovered something that would change her life... her teacher, a pretty brown skinned woman with what seemed to be one of her favorite dresses, was about to enter... it was a blue and black wrap around form fitter with a slit in the front... she enters the room, commanding the attention of the students... as she walks up and down the aisle, the student is watching for just one thing... the view from the slit in her dress where she can see the inside of her thighs... that was it... the teacher found herself receiving xmas gifts from the student up until she graduated high school & she would often return to her old school to spend time... to this day, they remain friends, the teacher having no idea that she was the students first crush.

Who knew my inquisitive & creative mind, would lead me to this point? Welcome to my Hideaway. Here I'll expose you to my most sensitive, orgasmic, and erotic thoughts.

JLynn

Testimony

I can do all things through Christ who strengthens me

So, when I have issues, or the world is weighing heavy

I lift my head and raise my hands to thee

Your spiritual journey is one of great importance

It is best described as our personal relationship with God

Jesus is our help in ages past

We must remain conscious of our decisions and be steadfast

This journey to heaven, is one we work on everyday

Keep in mind the devil is very busy, trying to lead us astray

This is my testament to the great one above

When I am struggling trying to find my way, He shows me love

There are times when I feel lost & don't know what to do

But when I get on my knees to pray, He always pulls me through

I can do all things through Christ that strengthens me

Let us remember to give praises and glory to thee

J Lynn

We are the greatest of Gods' creations
Long withstanding throughout time
Thoughtful, graceful, loving, and kind
We are true to our word, but quick to give a piece of our mind
Since the beginning of time, we've carried the torch
Yet we're heavily underestimated, and toyed with for sport
We are the givers of life and the bearers of pain
Our love covers our family and friends like an umbrella in the rain
We are mindfully efficient, our strength unknown
Step aside men, because we are the true air to the thrown
Hold your heads high ladies, and let them know we're here
Have faith in our lord, and show no fear
Display your strength phenomenally, never settle or leave it be
For we are queens who deserved to be crowned
So live and love life
Be free...

Strength of a Woman

J Lynn

Hearts open, souls ready to receive
She saw me... the real me, when so many others failed
Burned thru me with her brownstones
Helping me reach my level, poetically & romantically
Running towards the light
It was her, she freed me
In search of pure bliss
Walking in the rain, waiting for the sun
Laying in her labyrinth gave me peace
Loving her brought serenity
The tranquility in her touch gave me clarity
She was worth all of my energy
All my strength, ideas & fantasies
She embraced me in ways I never imagined
This compelling, impulsive, unselfish feeling to be whoever she needed
I wanted to give her everything she'd given me and more
A space of happiness
For her, my Tribute.

Tribute

I know I say it all the time
But... it's true
I just want you
I wanna' be whatever you want
I just want you
I wanna' please you, do for you
Spoil you, care for you
Love you
Make love to you, be sensual with you
Or fuck you
If that's what you want
I just want you
Wanna' talk with & confide in you
See you & spend time with you
Take you out
Wherever you want, just to share space
Show you things you've never seen
I just want you
Not all of you, nor all of your time
Every now and then
Here and there
Just because... I miss you
I know you miss me & want me too
I just want you

My mind, doing hula hoops all the things I can do with you...

Your panties
You don't have to take them off
I take your fingers, then mine- together as we play in her
Consumed by pleasure
Now, take those same fingers
I suck on them, still feeling you
Sweet cream building
Wetter and wetter
My fingertips like soft feathers,
Then, eating your pussy thru your panties
Meeting your climax
Pure discovery...

Interlude

In the belly of peace
As serenity overcomes you in silence
The darkness
Personal and private thoughts make their way to the surface
From the hideaway
Reflections of ones being
The desire
The inner instincts
Resonating
Never spoken
Never coming to pass
All feelings withstanding
The depths of fear
Underneath it all
I remain steadfast
In the hideaway

Hideaway

Weak

This intoxicating feeling... Motionless and spellbound, that momentary glimpse, seeing her for the first time, observing her, I was instantly weakened, strong yet tender thoughts... I was intrigued beyond measure... I wanted to know everything about her... Wanted to have her, bending to my will, I saw her in ways even she couldn't imagine... Like a hunter in pursuit, she was mine for the taking... Seeking her submission and vulnerability, undressing her with my eyes, it was me she'd fall victim to, insurmountable pleasure, cerebral intrusion, she would allow herself to be debilitated by me, not fully understanding why, I was everything she didn't know she wanted... Drawn to me like a moth to a flame, weak... and wanting more.

Your eyes
When I look into your eyes
I see the freedom I've always wanted
Its peaceful, serene, yet paralyzing
Numb
When you touch me
When we kiss
I see all that I've dreamed of
The love I've craved
I can't explain it
This feeling that I feel
Being with you
Its more than sex
The being and becoming
The you that you were meant to be all along
Finding yourself
The evolution
You did that for me
You set me free

Freedom

Essence

At first, I thought she was normal
Then I realized that she reigned supreme in my thoughts
No matter where I am or what I do, I think of her
Sometimes she's on my mind all day & night
She's so hard to shake
I love everything about her
The way she feels, tastes, looks, & smells
She empowers me
Taking advantage of her in every situation
She's my personal mission
What's wrong with me
She makes me feel so energized & alive
I could never do without her
As much as I love her, I fear her
She knows she has the upper hand
She could break my heart & I'd love her still
One day I'll gain control
For now, she is the essence of me

Interlude

Can I be your slave...
Lead & guide me
Like a goddess, I worship you
On my knees for you, ankles east to west
To ecstasy, you reach your peak
You say you tryna' be good, but with me you're great
Those stars you see, like constellations
They spell my name, one letter at a time
To another galaxy when we make love
Pleasure filled visons and dreams
I see you as you see me, sex crazy
And wanting more, galactic orgasms
Drowning me in your sweetness
Quenching my thirst with every release
Engulfing myself in you, I am yours...

MAY3E, this is how it's supposed to be
This is our time, right here, right now
We were meant to be
Our paths crossed for a reason
You need me, and I need you
MAYBE, we can put our pasts behind us
So. we can enjoy our future together
Our past will play a big part in our success
It made us the way we are
And, will allow us to appreciate the good in each other
Happiness for us is infinite
MAYBE, you are my soul mate
I can show you things
Take you places you've never been
You'll see love through my eyes, as it should be
I'll make sure you feel me, every chance I get
Mind, body, and soul... I am yours
Everything I am, I'll give to you
So... MAYBE, one day, you'll be my wife
MAYBE

Fire & Desire

Like a blazing fire
Burning everything in her path
She is uncontrollable
We are but hollow trees in a dry forest
Coming thru in a rage
Ashes to ashes
Dust to dust
We are inadequate, merely pawns
Falling victim to her desire...

Come To Me

Let me undress you
Tell you what I want and what to do
Your sexy bra and panties
Gimme' those
Surveying your beautiful frame
Open your legs, let me see what's mine
On top of you kissing and sucking
Your supple breast before I taste
Slippery when wet
I feel you
You're breathing hard
Anticipating the pleasure
My tongue in and out
Gripping the sheets as u grind
Feed me, take it its yours
Bending and twisting your hips
Wrap your legs around my neck
Its my pleasure, pleasing you
Making my way to your G-spot
Tasting you
Your clit swelling in my mouth
Making love
No end in sight
Cum for me again and again
Just as I like
Leading you to ecstasy
Do as I say, and we'll be here all night

Interlude

Please understand my thought process...

Like a late-night snack, It's you I consistently crave

Often losing sleep, the thought of you wanting to share an intimate moment with me... well frankly its arousing. The thought of you thinking of me, your clit rising and aching for me, heat generating from below, going from wet to creamy, all with just a thought of me... frankly its arousing. Beyond measure, please allow me to be me in this moment of my thought, thinking of you thinking of me... your cocoon opening, we blend so well together... your pleasure moans, the rhythm of your grinding hips like white noise it's a constant comfort for me, it enhances my horny, for me I'd rather please you than anything else, dance baby dance for me let my tongue beat off your body to your rhythm for longevity, your orgasms form the hook of our song as we make love on repeat...

The Unknown

I don't know what to say
On one hand I do, then again, I don't
There is so much to be done
So much left behind
Where do I start
How will it end
What's next
For me, I'm unsatisfied
Unfulfilled
Tired
Perhaps on a different path
Love still remains
Although not the same
I feel lost
Unsure of the unknown

I wanna' eat, be fed
Mouthwatering thoughts
The things I can do
My prisoner you'll be
For me, unlike any other
Responding in ways unimaginable
You never considered
Being with someone, like me
Pushing you beyond your limits
Perhaps, not having any at all
Depleted of energy
Helpless
To me... your pussy... is mine
Feed me

Feed Me

Goodnite

I wanna' sleep in it
Lights out, bed time
Lay between your thighs, nice and cozy
Covers over my head, getting' comfy
Mouth open, tongue out while I'm in it
Spread your lips, good night kiss while I'm in it
Hands under your butt, finding that spot
Sweating it out, it's so good
Legs locking me to the mattress
Hands stabilizing the flow
Reaching for your climax
Straight up cardio while I'm in it
Pillows all over the bed
Soaking up the sheets
Pressing against the headboard
Cumming so hard, with precision
Screams echo
Scents of passion fills the room
I see you
Make me work for it
I wanna' feel all of your love muscles
Bury my face in you
Hold on tight while I'm in it
It's so amazing, you tap out while I'm in it
Leaving me only to say, Good night.

There you were
Standing there, all alone
You didn't even see me watching
Mesmerized, I stood admiring your beauty
I wanted you, but
I often wondered if you would even notice me
Ever accept me
Allow me to be in your presence
With you
Patiently, I wait for our paths to cross
Day by day
Year after year
Cut from a different cloth
Beyond my realm
Perhaps
Is my very existence beneath you
Or, are my expectations too high
I don't want to let go
The fear of never having you
Is worse than I could have imagined
I guess I'll never know

First Glance

Interlude

Entering your space romantically, fingertips tickling enticing you. My soft lips, warmth of my mouth, and depth of my tongue... In search of something. You are beautiful... exploring your skin, massaging your hands, we hold tightly to one another... In my ear, breathing heavily, and often... surpassing your body, reaching your heart, melting into your soul... making slow passionate love... Close your eyes, can you see it...

Lovemuscle

How does it feel
Senses are heightened
With the slightest touch
Your completely aroused
The initial thought
Stroking your love muscles
The tension in your neck as we kiss
You grip my head, lick my lips
Suck on my tongue
Damn, I feel so greedy
I wanna' love on you all the time
The strength in your hands
As we touch, your fingertips
Gently... all over me
Your legs on my shoulders
Wrapped around my neck
Thighs comforting my face
Your climax is near
Feet on my back
Toes curling against my skin
Hands around your waste
The muscles in your back
Tightening with every stroke
Like a perfect storm
Abs tight, core shaking
Kegel muscles clinching
Around my tongue, you cum... hard
Gasping for air
Hold on to me
I'm gonna' make love to you

All night long
Just so I can feel your love muscles

lovemuscle

Journey

There you are
I've been looking for you
Waiting for this day, to set my eyes on you
You are the one that was made just for me
The love that you have for me is unparalleled
We've experienced similar things in our lives
And are very much alike
We have a lot in common
This is unbelievable
I'm so excited about our future
Let me give you a tour of my heart
There is so much I want to share with you
I promise to give you all the love you need
I'll be caring, compassionate, patient, and loyal
All that I am, I'll expose to you
We will live our dreams and aspirations together
Let me give you all of me
All I ask, is all of you in return

Seeing you today, your beauty and grace
I love making you smile, it makes me happy
That I can do that for you, even for a moment
I wish I could hold you, be beside you
Getting lost in your eyes, feeling what you feel
For me, sharing my feelings for you
My love for you, is undeniable
Unwavering, uncontrollable, everlasting
I love you so much, I miss you
Just that much, more than you know
Wish I could show you, everyday
Every hour, every moment
If you'd let me, for as long as you want
I'd like that very much, to give you
All of me, to show you
Not just sometime, but always
It's so hard caring for you and not being
Able to give it to you
Love is a powerful thing, an immovable force
I just want you to have it
All that I am, is yours
I'd love to share it
With you...

Interlude

Laying still
So warm, so peaceful
Touching you slightly
My fingertips from your neck
To your chest, down the center of your body
I think I'll have a sip
Stirring up the flavor
Probing with my tongue
Not rushing my flow
Sipping slow to quench my thirst
I can feel it, the tremble in your core
The shiver from inside
I just want a sip...

Distance

I can feel your presence
We're close, yet so far apart
Often, I think of you
Our spirits, united as one
We share the same passion for life & love
I wonder if you can sense my existence
So many have come & gone, but none of them like you
Sometimes I dream of you
What a pleasant thought
Knowing there is someone made just for you
They will compliment you in every way
The longing for love is overwhelming
But patience is a virtue
I feel like we are worlds apart
The distance makes me want you more & more each day
You are worth the wait
My distant love

Taking me wherever she goes
The excitement
Being around and near her
She has no idea
No clue how bad it is
Being my addiction
I think of her all the time
No matter when or where I am
She's always with me
Not just that mouthwatering wetness
But, her presence alone
I want her so bad... all to myself
I could spend hours and hours with her
And still, not be satisfied
Still be hungry, still wanna' feed
Wanting to share space with her
Without boundaries
She is my hearts purpose
My soul's satisfaction
I wonder if she gets tired of me
Pussy aching, clit throbbing, body sore
Needing space
From me and my appetite
I wonder what's it's like
For her, the object of my desire
I'd give, do, and be whatever she needed
Her pleasure is my happiness
The yin to my yang
Get me high, set fire to my heart
Let me go for a little while
Then pull me back in
I'll wait...

Interlude

Gently she welcomed me as if I'd never left. She missed me, how sweet of her, like a baby mouthing all over me. I love how she loves me, we speak our own language. I wanted her to know how much I missed her too... rubbing my face all up and thru. We needed that moment to ourselves. You were quiet at first perhaps getting reacclimated to my tongue. Once you reached for my head, I knew you'd found your rhythm. Looking down at me with a smirk... I know what and how you like it. I noticed you were trying to hold back a little, denying me... perhaps you'd forgotten how we got down, sweat dripping, gripping my head with the covers working my stroke... you're legs spread wide, you pulled me in close as you came all over me... you taste so good. It's good to be missed.

Soul Seduction

Let me give you an introduction
This is my personal soul seduction
It's funny how matters of the heart we follow every day
There is a force deep within, and it's the only way
We learn as young ones to follow our hearts
True, sincere, real love, is when the seduction starts
You find yourself isolated in one place or another
Its written all over your face, you can no longer keep it under cover
We find ourselves so deep, we can't even think
Some get it so bad, losing parts of themselves
What do you do when love reaches its peak
Try to stay cool, try not to speak
The soul as taken over and won't let go
Control your emotions, keep then on the low
You'll do anything to keep things tight
Don't ever let love go without a fight
Is there more to life than love
Besides our heavenly father from above
Your heart feels flooded, how can this be
You're locked in your soul's seduction, you'll have to wait and see

Inside my cocoon
Passion surrounds you
Engulfing your body
Isolating your mind
Seducing your soul
Cerebral ecstasy
That's where you'll find me
Waiting for you
Yearning for you
Put your trust in me
I promise, I won't abuse it
Let me nurture your emotions
Don't hold back
Feel the warmth
From within
My oral fixation
As you melt
In my mouth
Our chemistry is perfected
As we give into each other
Just be...with me

Belittle

An Intimate Lay

The warmth of your lower abdomen
Softly on my neck, I lay
Feeling your pulse through your inner thigh
Finding refuge in your vaginal heat
I feel free from the world, cradled and safe
There laying with you
Intimate comfort

Your love breathes life into my heart
I no longer feel heartbroken & unworthy
The tears I shed are of joy, not pain
You have helped me restore my faith in love
And, showed me that being in love can be easy
Loving you brings happiness to my spirit & peace to my soul
If good things come to those who wait
I would've waited forever just for you

Forever

Interlude

I wanna' fuck you so bad right now
I could so eat the hell outta' your pussy
Spread your legs so fuckin' wide
And just dive in
The complexion of your thighs and my skin
We blend perfectly together
You grab my head as I sink in
The wetter you get, the more I slide
In and out, around and around
Your cupcake icing is thick
And so damn sweet
I just wanna' live in your pussy
And frequently visit your ass
I'm so horny for you
Imma' work you out like a cheerleader
You'll yell and scream for me
Stretching beyond the norm
You'll feel the length of my tongue
The strength of my arms
As I grip your thighs
Long stroking, sucking on your clit just the way you like
Damn, I wanna' fuck you so bad!

Prelude

I'd do almost anything
To feel your hands
Holding me
Feeling your face on mine
On my shoulder
Kisses on my ears, face, and neck
I'm easily aroused by you
Just a quick glance
Instantly, I'm weakened
I can feel the anxiety
Even still, after all this time
You get nervous and shy
Like its your first time
Your skin is so soft
Body language timid
You're ready, but
You know I won't rush
I wanna' enjoy every second with you
Your temperature, is warm
And getting warmer
Just let me be here, in the moment
With you before we indulge
In the amazing

Something new

With a sudden rush of energy, you appeared
Not knowing what was about to happen
You came forth
Stepped in
To give me what I needed
What I've been waiting for
To fill that void of passion
The impossibility of progression
Prohibits me from true exposure
I will however be what you are to me
A confidant and friend
Your bodies hiatus from the norm
And, a fulfiller of your unspoken fantasies
For that I am thankful
Excited even
I look forward to sharing energy & space with you
I hope your ready
For something new...

You're the one they want
When we walk into a room, its you they're looking for
I'm just a shell, the one they see first
The one that holds you down
And believe me, it's not easy
If they only knew
If they could see you as I do
Charismatic... So gentle, yet assertive
You know just what they want
They feel special around you, important & loved
Your attentive and observant too
You can tell them things about themselves they didn't even know
You see what they don't
You're the emotional safe haven
The Kegel crusher
This intense burning desire, for them
You're their provider, their friend
Even though they'd never admit it, it's you
You're the one they want

Why...
Do I do what I do
Because of how I feel
I love you, I'm in love with you
Never met anyone like you
A cool, down ass, free spirited chic
Classy, sassy, fine as hell inside and out
Definitely out, of my mind
Like a fire set from within
All I do is think about you
I see you in everything
I treat you, like your mine
Talk to, tongue you down, spoil you
Like your mine
Always looking excited to see me
You feel for me, touch me
As if I'm yours
Although you won't express
Often, we lock eyes
In that moment, we know
You deserve it, that and more
I want to always be there for you
If you let me, you'll always know
That I got you
My friend, my love, & my vice
I am hopeful and helpless
Loving you is pleasure and pain
You have a piece of me
No one has ever had
Shown me things, I've never seen

Why... do I do what I do... simple
You've given me the Freedom, to just be me.

Again & Again

Here we are
Again...
You have failed us
My quest to please you
Always leads to this point
The pain
The emotions
It's overwhelming
When am I gonna' learn
Picking up the pieces
Again...
I swear
I hate you with a passion
Bringing out the best in me
Good when you're good
When it's bad it's bad
Losing sleep
Losing tears
Losing myself
In you
You're draining me...
I can't control you
And what's worse
I'm not sure if I want to
You're a part of me
Like it or not
Wishing you didn't make me feel this way
Again & Again

Abundant Pleasure

Let me massage your body from the crown of you head /To your fingertips /To the base of your spine /Down to your toes /I wanna' lick and suck on your supple breast /While feeling my way around your beautiful body /Spread your thighs for me /As I make my way between your legs /I love the way you squirm as I nibble on the inside of your thighs /I love how you giggle when I touch your tickle spots /As I part your lips and breath, you let out a sigh /I know you're ready / Your pussy is so well groomed, just the way I like it /I slowly begin pleasing you /Roaming the walls of your pussy like a hall monitor /My tongue circles every inch of you /Your walls start to moisten with every stroke/ Damn you smell good /I've been waiting for this moment for some time now /I grip your ass while eating your pussy /Moving your hips from side to side /I want to taste all of you /Stroking you from your clit to the opening of your vagina /I love the arch in your back when I take slow sips of your pussy /Your body is in complete control /Open your legs for me baby and pull your lips back /I wanna' have a full view of you /I want every drop of you /Let the wetness flow as I feast on you /I bet you've never had anyone want this pussy as bad as me/ I gently grip your waste and turn you over /Grab the headboard and brace yourself /I want you to sit on my face /Get into that frog position and lower your pussy /Ride me baby, any way you like /I wanna' feel the bed move as you gently bounce up and down on my face /Do what you please /It's all about you /I reach up to pull your nipples while pleasing you /I can see your sex faces /I can see you gripping the headboard while biting your bottom lip /Wondering how long you can last on top /You're so fuckin' wet and I love it /I can hear you moanin' /I can tell you're holdin' back /You don't wanna' give me the pleasure of hearing you call for me /But, you like it / As I slide from under you, I grip your waist and kiss your back /Down to your ass I go /Oh no baby, it ain't over /Get on your knees and ease that ass back /I got somethin' for you /I nibble, bite and run my tongue down your ass as I massage your clit from behind /You buck your ass back at me from the pleasure, as I taste you from behind /You return to your back /I palm your ass and pull you into me /You lift your legs high towards your chest /You reach down, grab my head and pull me into you /Feed me baby /I want it all /I can feel your body start to tremble /Your essence smells like fresh rain / You're ready to cum /But, you'll cum on my terms /I slowly lift you and stick my tongue in your pussy /As you begin to cum /You call my name /Oh, J... take it baby, it's yours /That's how I like it /And believe me, I'm gonna' take it all /Oh baby, you taste so fuckin' good /Like soft serve on a hot summer day /You continue to cum one after the other /I feel your stomach muscles, ass, and pelvis tightening /This is 69 by J /6 times you come /Then 9 more after that /I think I got it all /You take a deep breath /As I continue to tease you /I've dreamed about this moment /I know you have too /I've pleased myself at the very thought of it /I have wanted this for you and me, from the first day we met /Thank you for allowing me to be in your presence /Pleasing you abundantly...

Interlude

Sitting here, thinking of you
Mind just running
All the things I wanna' do to you
Slipping you out of some sexy underwear
Sucking on your breast
Listening to your heavy breathing
Slowly, taking my time
Kissing you from head to toe
Massaging your legs as I part
The warmth from your inner thighs
Your just as ready as I
Locking your hips in place
Tasting, rolling my tongue
You're soaking wet
Tightly you hold onto me
Pleasing and playing in you
Finding your spot
Yes, baby yes, there it is
Twisting and turning, it's so good
To the side, from behind, on your knees
Under the covers
My tongue, pleasing you again and again
I find your G-spot
Your clit, sensitive to the touch
Grinding up to meet me
Your front row seat to love
Watching me, as I devour you
I see you want more
As much as you want, feed me baby
Your body explodes from within

And out, you climax
I slurp and suck
Cum... cum for me baby
Ooooo damn, get it, work me
Give it all to me...

...Interlude

In The Clouds

Can I float and fly high with you
As we make love in the clouds
We'll inhale the air of passion
Exhale sounds of ecstasy
There will be no stress or worries in the clouds
Just time and space for us to enjoy each other
While engaging in emotional and physical affairs
Our bodies intertwined
Your touch is as soft as cirrus
Sensitive, provoking intense erotic movements
We'll enjoy pleasure to the utmost
Sharing love with one another in the clouds

I did it
Because I knew I'd be the only one
To have you
You were my virgin & I was yours
So openminded
So willing
So down for whatever
You allowed me to experiment
My deepest fantasies
Brought to life
Every time I touched you
We discovered new things about each other
I gave it to you
All that I am and always wanted to be
I found with you
It was at that point, I knew
A part of you would be mine, forever
I wanted to reach you in ways no one else has
I had aspirations of you feeling me
Weather we were close or miles away
Thoughts of US would excite you
To no end... you'd always want me
Want that feeling
Rarely showing resistance
Loving every bit of it
You became JAYded

On The Run

Sitting on the side of my bed last night, I was thinking where the fuck was she going... I thought this was what you wanted... you knew what it was before you came... removing the headboard and pillows... I wanted you to get all of this... scratches on the wall and my back... I was all over you, kissing on your tattoos, your neck, ears, licking down your spine... grabbing your ass, flipping you over, biting on your nipples, fingering your pussy, you moaning loudly unsure of what it's gonna be like... Massaging, kissing your feet, spreading your legs, gripping your ankles... where are you going, don't run... I haven't eaten all day so you bout' to get it, sucking on your lips, you're so damn wet, my hands and fingers- like soft cotton you feel so good in my arms, nahh' I ain't makin' love, imma' fuck you like I own you... wrap my lips around your clit, pulling, slurping, sucking...my tongue so long, you feel me from your pussy to your ass, flip you over eat you from behind, stick my finger in and eat your ass at the same time, damn I feel you cuming hard- so hard, squirt at me put it in my face, it's ok cuz' imma' get it all... oh, you didn't know- I don't get tired... pussy is so good I had to sit you on my face, looking up, watching you struggle, your arms outstretched, screaming as I drain you, calling my name hoping I'll ease up, "take it easy baby your killin' me"... Nahh', imma' make your pussy mine... every time you see me I want your pussy to get wet like instant grits boiling from the inside cuz' you want me to get it, want me to pick you up and sit you on my shoulders while I eat it... damn, don't run... where the fuck you goin'... imma be in your ass all fuckin' night... that's what I'm talkin' bout'... fucked you so good, got you running from the tongue... damn, I had her ass on the run... but she'll be back, for sure.

Burned
By the rapture of my own love
Up in flames, my soul, my heart
A love that I'll never have
My tears on the page, trying to put out the fire
Burned by my own will
The heat is overbearing, in a chamber
The never-ending feeling
I wanna' let it go
This burning deep inside
It is LOVE.

Burned

Addiction

Be the victim of my addiction
Allow me to take my frustrations
Out on you
It's impossible to overcome
Unrestrained passion
As you lose yourself in me
With me, there's no end
Pleasure seeking
An uncontrollable force
Sporadic and erratic
Erotic, my desire
To have my way, any kind of way
You are my mission
Surrender your fears
Let me devour your wants
Swallow your needs
Stay with me
Submit to me
Feed me
Let me share it with you
My addiction

As thoughts of you run wild
In my head, I am consumed
More often than not, I have visions of us
Expressing, experiencing, partaking together
Tasting your essence is like a window to your soul
Every time, I see something different
A new outlook on you, on US
Feeling what you feel
I am as much a part of you, as you are of me
Your legs provide comfort and peace
Our kisses and hugs
When we're holding each other
With every stroke, as I'm sure you do
I feel our love
I miss you already
Touching every inch of you
From the crown of your head
To the beauty mark on your feet
Pleasure brings constant showers
As you cum, over and over and over
From multiple angles
She and I
In perfect harmony
We make sweet music, while making love
You are mine, I am yours
We are one
As we indulge together...

Indulgence

Then Came You

How can a playa' that's played so hard, be so deprived
I've shared in the greatest of pleasures
Indulged in every desire imaginable
Many have come & gone, some willingly, others victims
None of them could've prepared me for you
The majority of my expeditions have benefited greatly
From the joys of being with me
I can't honestly say that it's been reciprocated
My intuition has often led me astray
There's always been something missing
My heart has longed for the fulfillment of love
I patiently anticipate the completion of this long journey
I want for myself, what I've given to others
I feel like I've paid my dues to karma for all the wrong I've done
I'm finally ready to claim what's rightfully mine
The love that God has made in his image just for me
Then came you...

Desire

I remember when you first said no
You said you'd never would
But, your body said different
Even though you had never been with a woman
You were oh so willing to let me have my way
As I stood facing you, I undressed you with my eyes
Preparing for what is about to happen
You want it so bad
Body lusting for someone to caress & embrace its sexual being
I stared into your eyes seductively, waiting for your approval
I wanted to hear you say it
Say that you want it & wanted to share it with me
I reached for you, trembling and nervous
What if it was better than what you're used too
How would you react to him
Would you imagine my hands, stroking your body
Would you imagine me tasting you
Looking between your legs, seeing my face
Thinking of all the orgasms you could've had
Miss what we had because, I know exactly what you like
Pampering that craving
Satisfying your desire

BrownSuga

Came across this chic who was mad curious
Not sure what she was expecting tho'
Stepping to me like I was the status quo
Like I was less than comparable to what she already had
She wasn't ready...

Had no clue what I was gonna' do
To her, she thought it was a onetime thing
The exposure was mind blowing
I had the pussy in a vice grip
I mean, it was on lock
Every time she saw me her whole world stopped
Legs start to shake, knees get tight, pussy gets wet
And her breathing was always slow and steady
She wasn't ready...

Man, if curiosity killed the cat
Then murder was definitely the case
She not only had 9 lives
She had 10 or 11.
I had her everywhere
My car, her car, front seat and the back, parking lots, the beach, on the stairs
On the bed, on her back, on her side
Licking the booty and eating from behind
We had that head grabbing, hair pulling, neck jerking, sheet biting, pillow throwing, mattress gripping, name calling, pleasure screaming, back arching, hips swivelin' kinda' love
With me looking up at her and her down at me
She said that pussy was mine
She wasn't ready...

I guess I shoulda' warned her huh
That my tongue IS the truth
That I'd be the best she ever had
That she'd get turned out
But even still
She wasn't ready...

BrownSuga'

Tic Toc

Minute by minute, hour by hour
I wait, eager to hear a word from you
Moving in slow motion, time
A matrix in which, my thoughts revolve
Counting tears as they fall from my face
Looking at my phone, hoping you'll call
Phantom rings I hear, in anticipation
Pacing back and forth from the window
Car after car, maybe you'll come by
I hear knocks at the door, it's just the wind
Wish it would blow this pain away
If loving you is the hardest thing
Then missing you is the infinite epitome
Sun shining out
But, inside its cold
Like the other side of my bed
I feel a quiver, yearning for your touch
Shared conversation, feelings invaded
Your scent lingering
Like counting sheep, no sleep
Instead I count precious moments
Now filled with the emptiness
Reading old messages of what used to be
Not being able to see or hear from you
I often wonder, do you think of me
Miss me, still feel for me
In your silent moments, cry for me
Minute by minute, hour by hour
So slow, creeping by
Leaving nothing behind

Just time
TicToc...

TicToc

Sanctuary

I sit and think
About my love and admiration
For pleasure
At the same time, I fear it
Satisfying my desire
For that one thing
The drive, the control
I love it, pussy
It speaks to me
In the most intimate way
Being between her legs
That's where I'm comfortable
I feel safe
Just she and I
The way she responds to me
There's no greater satisfaction
Showering in her wetness
Slow sippin', stroking, slurping, sucking
Her lips on mine
Having my way
Its personal, our connection
When I'm around
My presence excites her
Sending unspoken signals
She wants me, needs me
That feeling alone drives me crazy
Having knowledge
Her desire for me is just as strong
If not stronger
Her energy

I can see it, the way she walks
The looks she give me
When she's near, showing restraint
It motivates me
Triggering naughty thoughts
Being without her
Heightens my desire, my love
For her.... my sanctuary

Sanctuary

BodyWork

As the sun sets
So, rises the moon
Enhancing your silhouette
We lay claim to love
I am famished & eager to taste
Walking perfection
A piece of art so rare
You are- incredible
Like sweet caramel & butterscotch
You stick to my tongue
Addicted & wanting more
Having you, watching you
The way your hips move, that sexy moan
Loving the way you cream & scream for me
Relishing the opportunity
Savoring every bit
Of you, my priority
You grind as I kiss your neck, down your spine
Parting your ass I lick, pussy I eat & slurp
To your clit I suck, then back again
From wall to wall, you call for me
You cum for me...
Pulling on your nipples, you feed me
I am your bitch, I live on my knees
You undress my thoughts, fuck my brains out
My creativity is your greatest pleasure
Your wish is my command
Whatever, whenever, and however you want
I just wanna' watch your bodywork...

At FIRST GLANCE
It was SOMETHING NEW
Who knew I would discover my FREEDOM
It was you who LET ME OUT
And in that we found US
You chose to BE WITH ME
Feeding my ADDICTION
You received ABUNDANT PLEASURE
As we INDULGED in one another
EXPERIENCING the amazing
Comforted by your BROWNSUGA'
It's always been YOU
In my VISIONS and THOUGHTS
You SCREAM for me
Finally JAYDED
My pleasure pal

Interlude

I felt so privileged, she wore me like her favorite pair of jeans...my face imprinted, her body stuck to me like a candy wrapper, I felt her toes curling against my skin, her soft legs wrapped around my waist, heels digging in my back, hands and nails massaging my shoulders, entire body stretching reaching for her climax... it was right there, hers for the taking... my role was simple, pleasure... eating every inch of her, it's so good I can't help but wait... I want it just as bad as she... so warm, so creamy...

Comatose

I see you often in my sleep
Roaming around in my dreams
Even if I'm dreaming of something else
There are cameos of you
As I lie awake in bed, awaiting darkness
Inviting thoughts of you invade my cerebral space
Never willing to show your face
Makes sleeping so intense
I'm taunted with erotic fantasies
You make resting feel eternal
I am comatose

I submit to her always, SHE dominates my thoughts, ruler of my creativity, SHE is the one, surrendering to my desire for her, I am empowered, her essence strengthens me, SHE knows I'll do any and everything to please her, I love it, her smell, taste, and the way SHE feels, I fall victim to her often, my addiction her daily prescription, SHE made me, molded me, discovered this person I'd written about, seen as an unknown figure, from the shadows I emerged, between her legs, there I found freedom, SHE cries out for me, like a sweet silent whisper, to be in her presence, a feeling unlike anything I've ever felt, the art and beauty of making love, to her SHE may never understand, I see her everywhere, in my dreams, visions of having her, the positions, the screams, SHE with every experience, I become better than before, I can't shake it, nor do I want to, this feeling of only wanting her, being enslaved to her, pleasurable enshrinement, to her, to love and in love, I will always be... amazing- is- SHE.

Follow me
To a place you've never been
Let me show you
As my lips, heart, & hands lead you
On your body
Traces of me, all over
My touch, tongue, & kisses
Submerge yourself, in me
As I absorb
Your very being
I am your vessel of happiness and pleasure
Here, maximizing your potential
Love, as you've always imagined
It can and will be
With me...

Dejavu

Here I stand
Holding my heart
Pain bleeding into my soul
Beating so loudly
I can barely hear my thoughts
There's no peace, no serenity without your love
You freed me... now setting me free
Lonely and alone
This feeling, worse than the last
Loving you, harder than the last
How could this be
This sadness, I cry for you from the inside
Drowning with resistance to save myself
The fear of purging the tears
It's hard now, for me to look at you
Being so close, now so far apart
Love has abandoned me, again
Perhaps I'm not worthy
Of receiving as I give
Maybe I'm not deserving
Instead tormented
My need for affection & intimacy
Often evades me, with no regard for my feelings
Over and over again
It's DejaVu

You enter, and immediately our bodies are communicating... no spoken word, just US... We're sharing passionate kisses, hands all over each other... Feeling anxious by your presence, I undress you slowly but with pace... you're soaked, so I know I'm in your thoughts... Wasting little time, from your lips-breast- stomach- even licking and sucking on your fingers, I find myself face to face with her... your hands in my head, grabbing and pulling the way I like it... I'm eating your pussy, right there at the door... one leg propped up, and feasting... You begin to squat down like a catcher waiting on a pitch, legs shaking from the pleasure... on my face, as you sit and ride... wetness all around, you're screaming- I'm moaning... you hold me tightly as you begin to cum... nails in my legs as you ride faster and faster, cumming harder and harder, Damn, did I even lock the door

I Need You

Damn, it's like I'm always thinking about you
Wanting you
To be in your space & feel your energy
I love that you want it just as bad
It drives me crazy
Thoughts of you send me into overdrive
When I see you
You have my undivided attention
We impact each other in different ways
But, we're very much alike
Just putting it into words
Ughh...
I wanna' eat you right now
You're used to the love making, but
It's aggression that I feel
Roughing you up a bit
None of that gentle shit you're used to
I wanna grip, grab, and toss your ass
I can hear you
I'm all up and thru you
Eating your pussy, biting and nibbling on you
Teasing you
I'm in complete control
You come so hard, but I'm not stopping
No time for that
Imma' please you til 'you run dry
Then eat you wet all over again
Put it in my face
Pussy so wet, juicy, and drippin'
Damn, I want you to get it

I need you... oh baby... I need you

...Three

Miles Apart

There are days when I need to hear your voice, feel your touch
Days when just a glance of you is priceless
Sometimes I can feel you
If I listen hard enough, I can hear you
Your thoughts, whispering softly in my ear
I know you think of me
The distance between us is vast
Our wants on opposite ends of the spectrum
But our needs are the same
We're so close, yet miles apart

Missing You

I find myself starring at my phone
Waiting for your text
Or call
Just to hear your voice
I can see you
Feel you
When I close my eyes
You're there
Smiling at me, caressing me
Starring into your eyes
Kissing you
Holding you
Our time spent
SMH...
I'm missing you
Like it was yesterday
The moments we shared
The intimacy
The closeness
I'll never get to hear you yearn for me
Moaning my name thru pleasure
Enjoying me as I'm enjoying you
SMH...
I'm missing you
Every song I hear now, reminds me of you
At first you were ready
Now you're missing
In action & I'm sad
Will it ever go away
What do I do

With these feelings
The pain
I'm tired
My heart's heavy
SMH...
I'm missing you...

missing you...

Feel Me

Feel me, the energy
Rest your head on my chest
Hear my heartbeat
My pulse races
The closer I get to you
Sharing space with one another
Wrap your arms around my neck
Legs around my waist
Our body heat
Listen, inhale as I exhale
Passion and intimacy
I wanna feel you
Every inch of your being
In perfect harmony
You are the inspiration of my expression
A true guiding light
With every passing moment
The time spent
Together, we are one
Can you feel me...

It's too bad I'm not your type
The type to give you love, the kinda' love you need
The type to hold you down
The type to give you whatever, whenever
The type that gives you goose bumps on site
The type to make you smile
The type that puts you first
The just thinking about you excites me type
The when I touch you, you bite your bottom lip type
The sweet nothings that make you melt type
The take care of you type
Yeah, that's too bad
Too bad I'm not your type

Make Up Sex

Hot, steamy, passionate love
That's what I'm looking forward to
Spreading you beyond measure
Bending your legs back to your ears
Tied up on your knees
Tasting you
From your sweet spot to the base of your spine
The long stroke
Cuming again and again until you pass out
That's how it should be
Spanking you for being so naughty
Cupping your cheeks
Sitting you on my face
Locking my arms in place
Over your legs, so your forced
To experience the extreme pleasure
You gasp, every breath feeling deeper
Than the one before... your orgasms
Feeling harder, you scream louder and louder
I hear you calling me...
What's my name
You grip the headboard
Your body shakes, jerking, you throw it at me
Sticking my finger in, stroking your G
At the edge of the bed, I grip your ankles
Assume the position, legs east to west
Drippin' cum, I suck it out of you slowly
Slurping from every angle
Torturing you with this tongue
Your pussy is so good

You like it... you like being bad
You love the punishment
Sweating out every cell in ur body
Grinding your pussy on my face
Pulling me in... over and over
Icing so wet and creamy
She's all mine
I love it, I love my naughty girl

More Of The Same

It's been a while now, waiting for a different response...still, nothing

You think I'd be tired by now

Going out of my way, doing this & that

My feelings on the crap table, its tiring

Loving you is hard, yet still I try

The filler responses, comments on the sly

Your heart saying one thing, head saying another

Its damn near madness

Trying to express myself this way, thru poetry

I don't know what else to say

By now, I know it ain't meant to be

I ain't gonna' front though, I fuckin' hate it

If that nigga only knew, he got what I want

No shade...if things were only a bit different, it's my dick you'd be ridin'

That's just how I feel

You should be my girl, I'm just keepin' it real

Instead it's just the same shit different day

Nothing new, just more of the same

I've waited all my life
To feel what I feel right now
It's funny to me, in a way
The love I've been seeking
Is very much a reality
You are everything I'd hoped for
All I've prayed for
My heart is somewhat speechless
I feel love lock
The possibilities for us are endless
I can only describe my feelings as outstanding
There is nothing I wouldn't do to make you happy
My hearts purpose & my soul's satisfaction
Both being fulfilled
Gods guiding light of love shines brightly
On us together as one
You and only you hold the key
To my hearts love lock

love lock

Interlude

Slipping into her whirlpool slowly not wanting to disturb the flow... she bubbled as I entered with ease... dove in, hot like a sauna, steam opening her pores... fully exfoliated, moisturizing every inch of my pallet... regenerating, she came as the force of my tongue collided with her body... the strength from the rotation, draining her again and again, reenergized by her continuous climax... upon my exit, I was rejuvenated.

Onlyblind

I am awakened by thoughts of you
The calmness of your voice, touch so gentle
I never wanna be without you
You're such a blessing
It's so hard being away from you
Overwhelmed with excitement
I miss your encouragement
Those last words at night
I've never felt this way before
Missing you like crazy
You're always on my mind

Here I stand in the mist, wondering where to go
Finding my way used to be easy
What is loves direction
Is that the path to follow
What happened to love
I'm not sure I trust it anymore
Love has led me to be lost in the mist
A place filled with darkness & a disturbing chill
I feel pain, sorrow, & loneliness here
The mist holds no hope or optimism for the future
Just a stagnant docile conclusion that I am lost
Until love withdraws the mist, here I stand wondering where to go

Pulse

I can hear it
It's so profound
As I get closer and closer, getting deep and faster
Lying between your thighs, I often listen
And enjoy the warmth and affect your pulse
Your breathing gets heavier, the pace quickens
Exploring unprecedented pleasure
The pulse reflects the emotions from within
Your soul, where the senses are heightened
Your body is ready to express and explode
Quivering from the depths of your pulse
You begin to relax
Your pulse returning to where it once was...

Visions

I see you... clear as day
Sitting next to me in a cozy dim lit room
Candles burning, music playing
You and I
Staring into each other's eyes
Playfully, we tease each other
Our noses rubbing together
Biting and nibbling on one another
Smiling and laughing
You giggle as we share kisses and hugs
I'm kissing and rubbing on your hands
You know I can't be near you long, without touching you
I miss you, I see you miss me too
It's obvious our chemistry
You'd think we've been together for years
Or at least it feels that way
I can tell what you're thinking with a simple glance
You read me just as well, knowing what I need and when
As I drag my fingertips up and down your back
I feel the goosebumps
My touch arouses you
I'm aroused as well
After slipping out of your clothes, I step back
So I can look at you... you're so beautiful
Gorgeous even, soft skin and hands
As you rub on my head and neck
You know what you're doing
There is a sense of urgency, for me
You want me to taste, to give you
The AMAZING

So, I do
Knees back, legs up, holding hands
We enjoy each other
I please you for hours at a time
You take it because you love it
Cuming back to back to back
I know what you like
I'm more than willing
And able, to give you what you want
For as long as you want
I see you, clear as day
Visions....

The prosperity of passion
Intense emotions surface
As we make love
You're feeling me as I'm feeling you
There is safety here
As we hold and caress each other
Enjoying the moment
Taking nothing for granted
Just me and you
Our hearts share the same beat
As we stare at one another
It is imminent yet silent
As we fall deeper and deeper
This thing we share
Known to be simply amazing
It is love

Quiet Time

I envision...

To my surprise, you walk thru the door

Greeting each other, we smile from ear to ear

We embrace, holding each other close

So tight, we melt into one another

We share passionate kisses, and roaming hands

It's so difficult, we can't stay apart to long

Holding hands, still sharing space

It feels so good, so right

We are exactly where I thought we'd be

Normally, not overcome by emotion

We wipe tears from our faces, your hands are so soft

Damn, I miss you...

Ironically, you hear one of your favorite songs playing

You push back at me, towards the stairs

And up, we continue to kiss

Never breaking contact

Your purse on the couch, shoes, then shirt to the floor

Licking your fingers, kissing your neck

Sweet nothings fill your ears, you giggle and exhale

Worshipping every part of you

Taking nothing for granted, feeling our energy

Your fingertips stoking my head

Your hands are warm as you hold me, kisses so soft

Playing in my hair, always making me feel wanted

I remove your bra, suck on your breast, while biting your nipples

You smell amazing

Nibbling down your sides, traveling down your tummy

To your belly button, the small of your pelvis

You flinch, turning slightly I enjoy you

The taste of your thighs, legs, and feet
Legs lifted up, panties off
The aroma of your love, so inviting
You're watching me, smiling
I place your hands on my head, giving you control
Going, doing, having the amazing... however you want
As we share these intimate moments
We make love...

Quiet Time

Remedy

Unpredictable yet consistent
That amazing love
Soothes and calms
Like nothing else
The perfect end to a long day
Like the ocean
The unknown
One thing's for sure
It's always wet
Your body adjusts
To the temperature
That burning sensation you feel
You want it
Beneath the surface
You need it
Lying awake at night
Touching yourself
Pleasure filled dreams
Visions during the day
The yearning from below
Leading you to one thing, love
Come to me
Remedy

Although Mother's Day is once a year
I celebrate it everyday
Words can't express the love I have for you
You are my best friend & confidant
I can always look to you for support in everything I do
Many days, the sound of your voice is what pulls me through
I can go on & on about how great a mom you are
I want you to know how much I appreciate you
Your spirit is powerful & love everlasting
Thank you for your tolerance, comfort, and for just being mom
I love you today & everyday

You

It's always been YOU
Neither one of us knew it, but it was
YOU, who unleashed it
A love so pure, so raw
Uncut and untamed
A fury so rare
Tailor made for... YOU
What you've discovered
Is truly special
It can be molded to fit your deepest desires
Your wants and needs
Not just physically, but emotionally
It's yours for the taking
I just wish
It was YOU who wanted US
The way I want... YOU

Simply Amazing

You're always on my mind
Do you want me
The way I want you
Perhaps you do, and I don't know it
I wanna' feel your hands all over me
Wanna' feel your kisses
The softness of your lips on my neck
Whispering naughty thoughts in my ear
You take my hands and my kisses
Using them for your pleasure
I want you to have me
Do what you will, fulfill all of your desires
My happiness, its simple
You, allowing me to make you happy
My needs are met
The love & attention I receive from your happiness
Don't worry about anything beyond that
Or what you think I need or deserve
US and what we've established
Is all I need
Getting lost in your eyes
Your big, beautiful brown eyes
They comfort me
They tell me all the things you don't
When you touch me, I can feel your hidden feelings
The experience, is further affirmation
Of the same
Is it even possible, to reduce such great chemistry
To nothing
I don't want to lose that part of US

I'll do anything, baby anything to preserve it
This thing we share, known only to be
Simply amazing....

If I could, I would surrender myself into you

Leaving a portion behind

I've had many thoughts and visions of you carrying our child

We would be great parents

Sharing the love we have between us with our little one

Raising her in the church

I would kiss your belly every day, showing love to our seed

I would wait on you hand and foot, making sure you are ok

Our extra bedroom would become a nursery

Full of colors, such as yellows, pinks, & greens

Shopping would have an entire new meaning

Buying baby clothes and supplies would be my new hobby

I would run you warm baths

Read bedtime stories to the baby, cuddling you both while you sleep

Doctor visits would be an adventure

Watching as she grows healthy and strong

He or she would be so beautiful

Born into our lives as we love and cherish

For the rest of our lives

These tumultuous seas
Where I reside
Some days barely floating
Drowning in my own thoughts
Overtaken by emotion
Searching for courage
To face it... the fear
Its sink or swim most days
The highs and lows
Moods swing like riptides
Seeking stability
In constant limbo
I often wonder if it's worth it
Fighting for my sanity
This cerebral asylum
My padded headspace
Stranded and uninvited
It's a constant battle
Raging Waters

Raging Waters

You Don't Have To Ask

I've been in love with you for some time now
I love everything about you
Your heart is so pure & rich
You love me more than anyone ever has
I get chills every time you touch me
My stomach does flips & turns whenever I see you
When we're lying together, the passion is almost unbearable
I couldn't ask for a better lover
I love your body in its entirety
Your smile brings light to my darkest days
The spiritual connection is awesome
Our conversations are always enlightening
You always find a way to make me laugh
And, you can say the sweetest things to make me cry
Your love has broken down many barriers
Helping me embrace my inner femininity
I truly believe you were meant for me
Now whenever it crosses your mind
You don't have to ask

As you lay at the foot of the bed watching TV, I figure I'll finish the foot massage I started. You've been stressed and not sleeping well, so that should help. It's always interesting, watching as you become aroused at the slightest touch. Drifting from your feet, up your legs, to your thighs... bending back in a puppy stretch, I've never been as close to the moon as I am right now... nibbling on your thighs, you bloom and graze softly, so wet quenching my thirst, palming, spreading, gripping, riding, mouth open wide, I want it all... its romantic, just wanna' give you a good stretch, share some luvin', and watch you sleep...

Interlude

Scream For Me

I wanna' hear it, I wanna' hear you
Tell me how much you love it
Can you feel me tugging on your hips
Gripping your pelvis, as I pull you in
My hands all over your thighs
Up your torso, playing with your nipples
While I'm pleasing you
Sighhhs... you taste so good
I love watching you, as you rotate your hips
You feed me, as if you're all I'm supposed to eat
Squirm like your insides are on fire
As your pussy extinguishes bodily fluids
To my liking, I lick-suck-and slurp up
Every drop of you
Your body shakes
To the rhythm of my tongue
You look down at me and smile
You know I'll stay, as long as you want
Or until you pass out from the joy of it
Ughh, damn I love eating your pussy
Hold me baby, put me wherever you want
Turn to the side, so you can grind
On my face, I'm soaking wet
And so are you
I feel your hands, traveling
As you grab hold of me
Cuming uncontrollably
C'mon baby, don't hold back
I love it
When you scream for me

What happened to what we had
I miss you so much
Why must things change
When I was younger, we were inseparable
You, my mentor and I, your protégé
As I became of age, I saw less and less of you
Now, you're a mere shadow of what was
The absence of emotion is apparent
You're different now
When was the last time you spoke the words of love
Or displayed expressions of acceptance
I am the same now, as I was before
You don't treat me or look at me the same
Your willingness to compromise is needed
I fear the future of our relationship is dim
If God is love, why don't you except me as he has
Your love for me is conditional, therefore I am unfulfilled
But... I still love you

Loveless

Still The Essence

Why must you haunt me so
Like an unwavering force
Taking shape in many ways
I'm possessed
No matter when, where, or how
You always make me feel wanted
I can't live without you
I'll never let you go
To touch, hold, and feel
Pouring my heart out, for you
I'm aroused at the very thought
Of having you, tasting you, loving you
You empower me, making me want to be better
For you
I'll do anything
To be in your presence
You always have and will forever be
The essence of me...

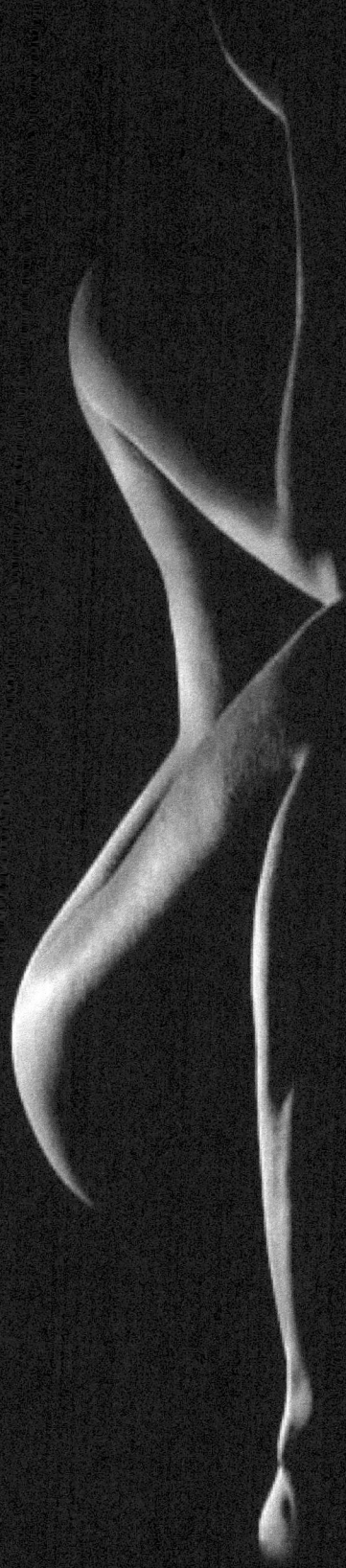

So Sensual

Have I ever told you how sensual you are
It's so serious, that I can feel you from near or far
You just don't know what you do to me
Maybe, I'll be blessed enough to have you eternally
Just the slightest touch drives me wild
I've even had dreams of bearing your child
Now, I don't mean to make you vex
But, believe it or not, it's all about sex
Most of the time, I like to feel you near
Holding me and spooning from the rear
I enjoy our time spent every day
Sharing my love w/ you in every way
Because of the sensual person you are
It's a major part that makes you my superstar
Sometimes you wonder why I'll do anything to please you
Just my way of complementing the sensual things you do

J. Lynn

Can I share a piece of my heart with you
Are you capable of loving unconditionally
Have you ever experienced love
Do you know what it is
So many have tried & failed
Stumbled, only to fall from the demands of my heart
I grow tired with every passing day
I want so much to be loved & have someone to love
When will I be blessed with the love my heart desires
Someone that is truly worthy
Of having a piece of my heart

Piece Of My Heart

119

Who's next

I need something
Someone who's gonna' be there for me
Who's gonna' wipe my tears
Hold me up when I'm down
Provide a smile to brighten my day
Or, maybe just a hug
I often wonder if she exist
The one...
Will I find her worthy
Of having my heart
Searching my soul for answers
Expectations are high
Will she be able to reciprocate
My feelings
I love hard, give freely, and to excess
How will I know
I often fear being alone
It pains me
So bad, crying myself to sleep
Imagining
It's her that rolls over to comfort me
Only to find its just me, I'm all alone
Who's next

Laying in the eye of the storm to the base of her cumulus clouds
The dew point is low, but the humidity is high.
Her hips directed my path, thighs articulated my thoughts
My language of love is rendered
The thunder began to roar from within, generating flashes of lighting
with my tongue
Expecting a torrential downpour
I felt the wind as she played in my hair, then came the rain
Saturated, I continued to dive deeper into the storm
I am drawn to the warmth and depth of the water.

Waterworks

What if I were yours & you were mine
In another place, at another time
The pleasure would be mine to share love with you
Your heart is so pure & true
You provide hope & ambition
Sharing love, for me is a great transition
Love is your hearts purpose & your souls' satisfaction
But if I were yours & you were mine, we would have no distractions

She had the all the right ingredients
My bed became her table and she my favorite meal
I could have her whenever & wherever I wanted, enjoy her
Taste her, savor every bit of her
Every day, or every now and then
Like leftovers, I knew just what to do to reheat and eat
She didn't seem to mind
Always admiring her goddess like frame
She always knows when I'm hungry
The way I looked at her, the soft stroke of my hand, the tone in my
voice
My day just wasn't complete if I didn't have her
So enticing, gives me butterflies as hunger builds
I crave her by smell, pleasure by sight, oral fixation by taste- hips
mixing- she feeds me, hearing her enjoying me & watching as I eat
The transference of heat as we kiss, biting her nipples, my lips moisten
as I get closer
So juicy, I lick from her sweet surprise- slurp to the base of her spine,
down her thighs
Licking my fingers- and hers cuz' I'm greedy like that
I'm her bottomless pit and she my ever so willing & ready favorite

favorite Thing

The Morning After

This morning, I arose to something beautiful... It was you
I could smell your scent in my sleep
It was as soft & sweet as a mid-day breeze
I really enjoyed you last night, but waking up to you is so much better
While you were sleeping, I had a chance to survey your physical beauty
From your silky hair, to the smooth surface of your feet
The texture of your skin melts in my hands like butter
I love the voluptuousness of your breasts & your rear is perfectly proportioned
The deep curve in your spine, reminds me of last nights' activities
I always wondered what it would be like, to just lay in comfort with you
Holding your body throughout the morning
Watching, as the sunrise glistens off your lovely frame
Your body is a piece of art, a sculpture gorgeously sculpted
If it had not been for last night, I wouldn't have had this opportunity
I'm glad I had the pleasure of being with you
The morning after

Part II
Now that I've set the mood and it's still early
It's time for you to get back on this tongue
You look so peaceful when you sleep
But... I gotta' do it
Since you're on your stomach
I'll lift one leg and gently slide under you
You're already wet
I hear you breathing deeply
So, I know your ready
Taking slow strokes, as I taste you
I can see you gripping your pillow
I hear you moaning
As your pussy gets wetter and wetter
You begin to grind on my tongue
Ride me baby, ride my tongue
Repositioning yourself, on all fours
Arms outstretched, Legs spread wide, back deeply arched
I'm gripping your thighs
I know your feeling me
Screaming obscenities
You taste so good
Oh baby, take your time
We got all morning...

The Morning After

Tell me
How do you really feel
About me and us
You've been so guarded
You show emotion, but rarely do you
Speak on it
I often want you to know where I am
Hoping that you trust me enough
To share the same
How do you feel, when you see me
Or when we're alone together
Tell me something I don't know
Deep down
Those unencountered feelings
The feelings you haven't admitted to yourself
I could tell you what I've observed, but
I'd rather hear it from you
I wanna' know
Baby please, tell me.

Miss Multipurpose

Not quite my girl, but she acts like it

My trap queen, she watches my back

Never having to look over my shoulder because she's always there

Like a finished product, if I'm good it's because she says so

She knows me better than most, the carrier of my deepest and darkest thoughts

We know each other in ways others don't, it's authentic

Bringing out the best in me

Keeping it real on all levels

You see, I'm a little bratty so she's hard on me

There's no getting what I want, only what she feels I need

Confident, hardcore and don't take no shit

She does her own thing, so I'm careful not to sweat her

When she wants that romantic nurturing vibe she knows where to go

Luvin' so good, when she puts it down it's always worth the wait

When we're doing US it's amazing, stress relieving, spontaneous, unlike any other

The best I've ever had

When spending time, she's the most important person in my life

I'm whatever she wants and needs me to be

I got mad love for Shawty

A big part of me, meaning more than she'll ever know

Holding me down, a true ride or die

That's my Shawty

Interlude

I don't wanna' be alone tonight... wanting you to come thru and chill with be, be with me, sharing and spending time... we don't even have to talk, I just want you here... looking upon your beautiful face, your soft big browns... I miss you... I know you said you don't want US anymore, but I can't help but think about you... I wanna' make love to you, to your mind, your body I can feel all over me... When we do what we do, its amazing... Our embrace... Not knowing what space you're in right now, you might not even be feelin' me right now... But I'm thinking about you... Please, please don't think less of me for wanting you the way I do... I wanna' be inside of you, traveling your thoughts, looking for me- in you...

Tasters Choice

Can I taste you
I have an oral fixation for your vaginal sweetness
The very thought of it makes my mouth water
Your pheromones drive me crazy
I love how your temperature rises when your excited
It's amazing, the reaction I get from just a simple kiss
I know that you think about it as much as I do
You think of me playin' in your hair
The soft touch of my lips upon your skin
I get closer to you
You feel my breath as I open my mouth to taste you
I look up, watching your body motion
It's already wet
Your body is calling me
Let my tongue do the talking
As it spreads your lips to taste
Damn, you feel so good in my mouth
I'm gonna' swallow every drop of you
As I stroke up and down, in and out
Slowly as the muscles on the inside start to tense
Your legs begin to shake
Your orgasm comes down, and exits
Like cotton candy, I can't get enough
Its pure pleasure
When I'm tasting you...

I can always tell
When you're feeling down, depressed, or deep in thought
Call on me
You don't have to bare your pain alone
I can do it for you
Lay your head on my chest
Let me do your worrying
I'm strong enough to absorb your fears, doubts, & heartache
I would take it all, if it meant seeing you smile
If it meant seeing you laughing & enjoying life
If it meant spending the rest of my life with you
Being a witness to your happiness
Being... your pain pal

Pain Pal

Dearly Departed

There we were staring into each other's eyes... that quiet space, neither one of us knowing what to say... I miss her...all I wanted was for her to caress my hands, up my arms and hold my face close to hers... I needed to feel her... wanted to hear her tell me how much she missed me and wanted to share space with me... in that moment, I could feel her hands all over me... on my back pulling me closer to her... cuddling as we share passionate kisses... then feeding me... if nothing else, I just wanted to hold her... wanted her to make me feel wanted... that very next moment, just like that... she was gone.

When the sun cries, darkness falls from the heavens
The heat is filled with gloom and despair
Nights are depressing and everlasting
The moon is sad and low
The earth, still
All that we know will cease to exist
Civilization is drowned in dehydration
Unhappiness wreaks havoc upon the world
The devil is busy
Desperation

Desperation

Losing

I'm losing
This battle with you
I try to play it cool, but
I feel like you're chasing me
Why must you be so demanding
Or, am I just weak
Truth is, I need you
I need you to need me
To want me, to love me
Tell me, how much you miss me
That you miss my touch, my kiss, my love
I feel alone at times
In my thoughts of you
Wherever you are
I need to hear it
That you think of me
Your intimate thoughts
Does your body cry out for me
I wanna' know
Want you to pour your emotions, into me
I'm losing it
At times I can't rest
Wondering if I'm on your mind
My need for your attention
To constantly be fed
It's crazy I know, but
I try, I try to play it cool
The need to be needed, emotionally
I don't wanna' be this way
Or do I

Thinking Of You

My favorite past time. Your beautiful smile, soft skin, and big brown eyes... to me you're perfect. I love how you see thru me & read my thoughts. You always know what to say. Your demeanor, your swag... it's like a direct line of sight thru the fog... like a whirl wind, its refreshing. Watching from below as the light hits your frame, your love resting comfortably, massaging your breast, you perspire slightly as heat rises from the soles of your feet to the crown of your head and exits ever so slowly for me to taste. Gently, you lean back letting out sensual sexual screams of pleasure. The amazing, phenomenally... It's all yours. There is joy pleasing you, taking care of you. Feeling me, feeling you. Your thighs on my face, like peaceful sleep on soft pillows... hands caressing every inch of you. It's important, reaching you on this level, our attraction to one another is undeniable. Making love to you, showering me with your orgasms, pulling grabbing, bury me... let me get lost in your pussy. You'll find me on the opposite side of 'Amazing'.

Come to me... I'm thinking of you

Inferno

Drifting out to sea, I submerge slowly into her volcano, we set fire to love, sparks fly, sweat drippin', comforted by warm sheets, her heels branded into my shoulders, my tongue blazes a trail of smoldering heat throughout her body, orgasms like hot lava, I embrace the undertow of her warmth... Inferno

It's crazy ya know
I was doing so well, then came today
Thoughts of you
Playing hide & seek across my mind
Every time I close my eyes, I see US
I see you sprawled out on my bed
Pleasure screaming, calling my name
Pulling my hair, palming my noggin
Pulling me into you, thrusting your hips
Grinding on my face, one stroke at a time
Your beautiful body, breasts and thighs
Hands so warm, hot even
Blood pumping, heart racing
Cuddling together, having pillow talk
Laughing & flirting
As tears roll down my face
In the moment, I miss you so much
Our closeness, I just wanted to hear your voice
Wanted to call you, just to say hi
Then I opened my eyes... It was just me

Imagination

The Experience

So soft
Like your favorite flower
At just the right time
I breathe, she blooms
Your body is tense with anticipation
Relaxation sets in, as does my tongue
Her essence is exhilarating
You exhale
As I begin to taste
She's naked and smooth
Just the way I like it
Blood rushes to the spot
Your excitement builds
I hear you, I feel you
Ur hands all over me
Massaging my scalp
I love when you pull my hair
Your cupcake is warm
Sweet to the taste
Melting in my mouth
With every stroke
You begin to tremble
I watch
Your hips rotate forward
Feet gently planted
In the bend of my shoulders
You rise up to meet me
Again, again, and again
Your expression of pleasure increases
You crescendo into your climax

It's so creamy
A reflection of your body temperature
You cum, all over me
Muscles pulsating
As I slurp, one release at a time
You hold & clutch me tightly
Like you, I love it... oh baby I love it
The experience...

...The Experience

Slowly

You gaze into my eyes , never saying a word, but you know I know...
slowly, I lick my lips to confirm your thoughts, smile to agree to the
terms... slowly, we breathe together and on one accord, like a magnet
pulling us closer... slowly, I reach for you, cupping ur cheeks I lean in...
slowly, putting my face in your neck, inhaling your scent... slowly, I
exhale rub my nose up your ears, my face against yours... slowly, I lick
and nibble on your lips... slowly, you dip your head back, kissing on
your chest... slowly, your pussy gets wetter and wetter... damn, I can't
wait to taste you... slowly, drop by drop inch by inch... Slowly

Often, I think of coming home to you
Seeing your smiling face when I walk through the door
I remember how it felt when you held me
Any and all thoughts of my day would instantly disappear
I used to have so much fun with you
Spending quality time, just me and you
Laughing, talking, and enjoying each other's company
What happened to the love
Our intimacy was awesome
I recall all of our extreme encounters
My body quivers at the slightest memory
Your fingertips sent shocks down my spine
Our bodies wrote perfect lyrics to loves hottest beats
Now, I barely remember the song

Faded Memories

Temptress

I see you every day, same time same place
Sometimes I catch myself looking for you, just to see you walk in
You're so sexy....
At first, I used to deny my attraction to you
Now, it's automatic
I even recognize your scent
Until now, I didn't know how bad it was
Being in your presence heightens my senses
Why haven't I said anything
Just thinking about it makes me nervous
My attraction is so much more than sex
I like everything about you
The way you carry yourself
You're self-confident, independent, & hella' sexy
A good woman, my type of woman
I often have thoughts of laying you down
Giving you full access to all your needs
Leaving only the sheets to tell the tale
Maybe one day I'll expose you to my thoughts
Until then, you will forever be my Temptress

Can you hear the sound of the heartbeat
It has the sound of desire, wanting, and yearning
For love and soulful passion
Feel the pain as the tears smear the page
The heart is lost for words
Not knowing what's in store
The beat is slow yet steady
Searching for what was and what is to come
What will be the fate of the heartbeat
Will it fade out and beat no more
In fear, filled with everlasting emptiness
The beat is hollow and still
I used to love what the heartbeat stood for
Now, I'm not so sure
The beat is slowly fading without motivation
To be as it once was
A heartbeat for love
Listen carefully and you'll hear it
As it comes to a complete stop, to love no more

The Possibilities

I wish I could tell you how I really feel
I wish I could tell how much I care for you
That I think about you often
Wondering what you're doing and if your needs are being met
I wish I was given the opportunity
To give you everything you want and need
To be the shoulder you lean
To free you of any heartache & pain
Is it possible that I'm the one your heart's searching for
Is it possible that I'm the one who was chosen to share your sacred love
Possibly...

I wish I could love you
I wish I could show you what it's like to truly be loved
Unconditionally & wholeheartedly
In a place where love has no limits
A place where you could leave all of your fears and reservations behind
To provide you with a new vision of how love should be
A place where you are treated like a queen all the time
You are placed on a pedestal all your own
Is it possible that I could hold a special place in your heart
Possibly...

I wish I could make love to you
Take you to a place you've never seen
A place where pleasure is provided by any means necessary
Making love to you... Mind, body, and soul
A place where pleasure is not only felt physically, but spiritually as well
A place where you can feel my hearts joy for pleasing you
A place where your love is honored and adored
A place so sweet, tender, and warm
Where your body is respected and cherished
Where no stone goes unturned & every inch of your body is satisfied
Where you can have all you want, where, and at any time
Is it possible that I am what your body needs
Possibly....

I wish I could give you all these things and more
If you knew then, what you know now... Would the outcome have been different
Would you have taken a bit more time, or even given me the time
Is there any possibility that we could be together one day
Possibly...

The Possibilities

Her&he

HER:

I WASN'T READY.......

I was curious of the unknown

Clueless to what I would find

There.....

What I found there was AMAZING

I wasn't ready.....

Thought I would be there for

A minute only just to see

But to my surprise I wanted

To be there for eternity

I wasn't ready......

My mind is scrambled with thoughts of being there

All the emotions there..

Wanting to stay there. I can't.

I wasn't ready......

A piece of me will ALWAYS be

There's no doubt, I ache inside

Knowing I must exit out.

I wasn't ready.....

ME:

It was me

Who wasn't ready

I didn't know I would fall

In your warm abyss

And find freedom

I'm able to be me

Showing expression in ways

I never could with others

You opened my eyes and heart

Loving differently

And in turn, you became my first

The innocence of this thing

The AMAZING

Taking it, my heart

Imposing your will

On me, then on you

This love, my freedom I was hoping

You'd keep for yourself

To build and nurture

It will always be, yours for eternity

Then you walked away

From me, from US

Indeed, it was me

Who wasn't ready...

Her&He

Interlude

Distant and broken, she was guarded... her heart was homeless, in need of affection and safety, like a pyro I controlled her flame, washed away her fears, as she showered me... introduced her to something real... it was worth it, I gave her time- attention- and much needed love... in return, she allowed me to break down her walls of hurt and lost emotion...

It's something about you
That makes me feel the way I do
It could be your beautiful smile
That makes my heart run wild
Maybe it's the curvature of your lips
Or that slow swivel in your hips
All I need is one chance
To expose you to the ultimate romance
Come and join me in my bed
Let me lay you down and spread your legs
I think I'm losing my mind
That sweet surprise is what I wish to find
Can I work that bangin' body of yours
Feeling your nails in my back behind closed doors
I'd like to play with your perky breasts
But inside your abyss is where I'll rest
Let's not forget about that sexy ass strut
Here, let me flip you over so I can slap that big ol' butt
I gotta' find me something to eat
But it's gotta' be vanilla sweet
I have an idea, so have no fear
Turn over so I can taste you from the rear
I wanna' see your honey drip
So I'll start with a slow sensual sip
Then I'll wrap my mouth around your world
So I can make your toes curl
Suckin' on your clit like a candy cane
Invading your space with my tongue awaiting the rain
I love the way your body quenches my thirst
It's hard to believe you were so shy at first

All we can do now, is hold each other tight
While sleeping so peacefully, after this magical night
I hope you enjoyed my style called "Unique"
Now you know what it's like to be w/ a real freak!

To The Clouds

As I look to the heavens, I see the staggered inconsistencies in the clouds.

What a profound moment, to know that even the clouds are mercurial

Still knowing that all things made by you are great.

It is our ways, tendencies, and behaviors that blemish this.

From birth, you've provided that blueprint.

It is important that we realize even with our imperfections that we are great

You Lord are great.

Only then, will we tap into you Lord

Through our spiritual relationship we'll achieve that blessed greatness.

Acknowledgments

First, giving honor to my Lord and Savior. Thank you, Lord, for the trials and tribulations of the past, present, and future. Thank you for giving me the courage to share my gift of expression. To my family, I love you all so much. I appreciate all your support. Thank you. To my Fantastic 5. Thank you all for being there, holding me down, hearing, reading, embracing my creativity, never judging, and always pushing me. To my counselor, thank you for keeping a stronghold on my mental health. To my BFF, we've been thru so much. I know it hasn't been easy. From birth, you've nurtured, loved, disciplined, encouraged, and now look... we're closer than ever. You are my rock. I love you Ma! To SloWriters Publishing, thank you for noticing and taking a chance on me. There are so many others that have reached me at one point or another. Thank you, thank you, thank you.

JLynn